UNMASKING
Sexual Con Games
3rd Edition

Unmasking Sexual Con Games
Teen's Guide, 3rd Ed.

Published by the Boys Town Press
Boys Town, Nebraska 68010

Copyright © 2003 by Father Flanagan's Boys' Home

ISBN-13: 978-1-889322-55-1 (pbk.)
ISBN-10: 1-889322-55-5 (pbk.)

The Boys Town Press is the publishing division of Girls and Boys Town, the original Father Flanagan's Boys' Home.

You can call the Girls and Boys Town National Hotline at any time with any problem.

1-800-448-3000

10   9   8   7   6   5   4

UNMASKING
Sexual Con Games
3rd Edition

A TEEN'S GUIDE to Avoiding

EMOTIONAL GROOMING and DATING VIOLENCE

by

KATHLEEN M. McGEE

LAURA J. BUDDENBERG

BOYS
TOWN
PRESS

BOYS TOWN, NEBRASKA

Table of Contents

What Is Emotional Grooming?

Dating and relating. Sometimes fun, sometimes confusing. And, for some teens, relationships can be dangerous and destructive. How do you know if you're in a good relationship? How do you know if you're in a relationship for the right reasons? Can you tell when someone is using you? How do you know if you're in over your head?

This book is designed to help you learn more about healthy as well as unhealthy dating and relating. The first several chapters focus on how to recognize and avoid an unhealthy or dangerous relationship. You will learn about emotional grooming and sexual con games – manipulative and dangerous behaviors that lead to unhealthy and destructive relationships. The last few chapters focus on healthy relationships. These chapters will provide you with the tools you'll need to create and maintain good friendships and healthy dating relationships, now and in the future.

Emotional Grooming

When someone manipulates another's emotions to skillfully gain control of that person, that process is called "emotional grooming." Emotional grooming is used to seduce, coerce, or "con" others into sexual activity. Grooming is a preparation, a process where the "groomer" – the person who tries to gain control of another person – tries to trick, convince, or coax his or her target into some form of sexual behavior.

Sometimes, these "grooming" tactics are deliberately and carefully thought out and planned. Other times, groomers merely mimic what they have seen, heard, and learned from others. In almost all cases, groomers don't know how to create a healthy relationship and usually have a warped and self-centered view of what others can do for them. They most likely learned their behaviors and other misinformation about relationships from peers, media, or adult role models. Most have never seen or experienced the mutual respect and selfless behaviors it takes to create a healthy relationship.

A Coercive Process

Regardless of the level of culpability, if the groomer is successful, the target usually ends up in a sexually abusive, manipulative relationship. The groomer attempts to control the target both physically and emotionally.

The process of emotional grooming can occur at any age. Young people who have not developed distinct and healthy personal boundaries are very vulnerable to a groomer's tactics. Many teens do not fully understand the psychological, emotional, and social impact of engaging in sexual activity. The emotional groomer attempts to teach them that premarital sexual activity is not only acceptable but also expected. The groomer uses seduction, bribes, or threats to teach this "lesson." Although targets may know something is wrong, the groomer establishes and maintains a position of power and authority.

Many adolescents who end up in such manipulative relationships were conditioned at an early age to "please" others no matter what. The groomer takes full advantage of this trait. Other targets are so starved for attention, for someone to care for and protect them, that they will ignore or dismiss the physical or emotional coercion and manipulation just to have a boyfriend or girlfriend.

Youth who fall prey to emotional grooming are often talked into doing things that are immoral or illegal just to please the groomer. Many times, young kids become targets because they aren't as physically or emotionally strong or aware of manipulation as adults or older youth. Many youth who are sexually abused are conned into believing that this is the way they should behave. They are told repeatedly that sexual activity is the way to show love, and they believe it. They are convinced that having premarital sex is expected and accepted, and is something they should do to earn love, acceptance, or status.

Learning about the tactics, cons, and lines used by groomers will help you figure out when someone may be trying to use and manipulate you. The first step is awareness. You need to know how to recognize the groomer's tactics and lines, and then use this knowledge to avoid being used or hurt by others.

The Power of Information

The information on emotional grooming is not presented to make you fearful of being manipulated or abused by everybody. You need to realize that there are many good and trustworthy people in your life who want what's best for you. You certainly can learn to develop healthy and wonderful relationships with other people. But the reality of today's world mandates that teens be aware that there are some people who are out to please only themselves. We don't want you getting emotionally or physically hurt by someone you believed you could trust.

Emotional groomers are manipulators. And some are very skilled. Some groomers will try whatever is necessary to convince a youth of the groomer's undying love and loyalty. Often, the target desperately wants to feel protected and wanted, and this desperation makes the groomer's task even easier. By the time a target feels or realizes that something is wrong, the groomer quite probably has enough control over the target to get what he wants.

Emotional groomers actually are perpetrators. The word "perpetrate" means to be responsible for carrying out a crime. And that's exactly what sexually taking advantage of another person is – a crime. The emotional groomer is the worst kind of thief. He steals a young person's youthfulness and happiness; he robs young targets of the innocence and safety to which they are entitled. He leaves his targets confused, humiliated, and ashamed.

The following material is designed to help teens understand how groomers go about emotionally preparing and shaping other people's behavior in order to use them. Teens should understand that the groomer wants control. Teens also need to know that there are ways to avoid these controlling sexual con games. The groomer is skillful in playing his game but that doesn't mean the target is powerless. The more a teen knows about how to recognize sexual con games, the easier it will be to unmask the groomer and see the game for what it really is.

Characteristics of a Groomer

There are no specific physical characteristics that identify an emotional groomer. A groomer can be male or female, teen or adult, a college graduate or a high school dropout. It's what the groomer does and says – his or her behaviors and words – that can alert a teen to the possibility of a con game.

Some people think that since males are typically more sexually aggressive that emotional groomers are always male. It is true that most sexual crimes – rape, sexual assault, and sexual abuse – are perpetrated by males. Yet, there are many females who use sexual con games to manipulate and get what they want. In fact, in some contemporary music and teen movies girls as well as guys are encouraged to be "players." Elements of contemporary youth culture actually glamorize, admire and respect players. The important thing to note is that a groomer or a target could be someone of either gender.

Emotional groomers may:

- Be male or female.
- Be a teen or an adult.
- Be well-educated or a high school dropout.

In order to remind the reader that a target or groomer could be of either gender, the text will vary the use of pronouns when describing both groomers and targets. Sometimes the groomer will be referred to as "he" and sometimes as "she." Likewise, the target will sometimes be referred to as "she" and other times as "he."

Emotional groomers sometimes disguise their con games with what seem to be caring behaviors in order to mask their real intent. For example, friends often give gifts to one another as an expression of how much they care. It makes the giver feel as good as the receiver. That's normal. The groomer, however, gives his target a present because he wants something in return. Every time he does something for his target, he chalks it up as something his target owes him. He runs a system of sexual debits and credits, and expects to be paid in full.

Groomers may be "slick" talkers. They may be skilled at intimidating others. They may have "status" at a school or with a group of peers. They may have money or access to drugs or alcohol. Regardless of how they play their con games, groomers take emotional and physical advantage of others.

Why Groomers Groom

How does someone become a groomer? Most often, it is simply a matter of imitating and mimicking observed behavior. Many teens groom because they believe that this is how you're supposed to act in a relationship – this is how you get the guy or girl you want; it's how you prove you're "macho" or "cool." Or, they believe that the purpose of dating is to get sex and the way you get sex is grooming. Perhaps they've seen grooming "work" for older siblings, parents, or other family members. Perhaps they've seen it glamorized in entertainment media and decide to follow that example.

There is hope for this kind of groomer. Although they have learned an unhealthy pattern of behavior, it is possible for them to learn new, healthier ways of relating. The difficulty lies in helping the groomer **want** to change. For many groomers, manipulating others has reaped pleasurable rewards, and therefore they are not highly motivated to change. Yet, change is still possible.

For a smaller percentage of groomers, their reason for grooming is caused by more serious and difficult life issues. This type of groomer is tuned in only to his own needs and desires, and is extremely confused about the true nature of friendship, love, and sex. Some may live in families where there is little love and care but lots of problems. They may have been severely rejected by parents or loved ones, and often they've been abused themselves. They may have suffered the pain of being used and are now using others. Most of these groomers have little or no knowledge of normal emotional, physical, or sexual boundaries. This type of groomer is most likely acting out of deep-seated hurt and pain and will need professional help to change. If you know someone with these kinds of issues, please encourage him or her to find a professional who can help.

Regardless of why groomers do what they do, the end result is that they hurt someone else. We need to dissuade groomers from grooming, and learn to recognize and avoid the hurt caused by falling for a sexual con game.

The Emotional Grooming Process

There are two key elements that the emotional groomer must have in place in order to successfully control someone else – a **false sense of trust** and **secrecy.**

False Sense of Trust

One element of the emotional grooming process is developing a false sense trust. A groomer convinces the target that he is the only person in the world who can really be trusted. The groomer swears that his life revolves around the target: *"You're all I think about," "You're my everything,"* or *"You're the only one who really understands me."* At the same time, the groomer also tries to convince the target that the groomer is (or should be) the most important person in her life: *"I'll always be there for you," "No one could love you the way I do,"* or *"I'll always protect you."*

The groomer also attempts to build trust by saying over and over that this relationship is good and natural: *"Everything is all right, don't worry, I'll take care of you."* The groomer usually does take care of his targets; he may buy them gifts, or protect them from others, or treat them with favoritism. The groomer skillfully connects much of what he does with the word "love:" *"This is the way it's meant to be. This is what real 'love' is all about."* The target is easy prey once she feels sure that the groomer is loyal and trustworthy, and is convinced of his "true" feelings.

Throughout this process, the target's loyalty is tested and the groomer's control is strengthened. After a groomer successfully weaves this web of false trust, his next step is to get the target to take part in some form of sexual behavior. The target is assured that premarital sexual activity is not only okay, but also the "right" thing to do.

In healthy relationships, trust develops slowly and gradually. Trust is not earned by simply repeating over and over again, *"Just trust me, baby!"* Trust is not based on the spoken word but on actions. It is through a person's behaviors, shown over time, that he or she proves worthy of trust.

The emotional groomer tries to rush this process and create a false sense of trust. The groomer is in a hurry to convince the target that he is dependable and trustworthy. The groomer will **talk** a lot about trust, especially telling the target why others should not be trusted, but allows no time for a real sense of trust to develop. In reality, the groomer is creating a false sense of trust. It certainly is not the trust that is present in healthy relationships. It is really an unhealthy dependence that is created by manipulation and deceit.

Teens who are hungry for attention and affection are prime targets for the emotional groomer. So are teens with poorly established boundaries. Such teens are eager to find someone they can trust, someone who will protect and befriend them. These teens don't have enough real life experience to recognize the characteristics of a real trustworthy person. They are easy prey for the groomer's lines and sexual con games.

This book contains excerpts from actual letters written by one teen to another. These letters illustrate how groomers go about developing a relationship with their targets. The following excerpts illustrate how the groomer tries to create a false sense of trust.

> "I just want to talk to you in private with no one else around so I can tell you how I really feel. I won't do anything else, I promise. You will know that I can be trusted when you get to know me better. I would never hurt you or anything like that."

> "No matter what happens to us I just want you to know if you need anybody to love or just talk to when you are down, I will always be available."

> "I'll treat you right and I'm not going to do anything behind your back. You are what I live for. So without you my soul is black and my heart is empty. It might sound like I'm trying to get over on you but I'm not. I mean everything I say. It comes from the heart. I cry almost every night hoping I could be with you. You're the best girl I ever had."

> "We can't let anyone break us apart. If we get into an argument or disagreement we will work it out. People here can't be trusted. Only trust me."

What makes these lines believable? First of all, a sexual con artist will say these things over and over. She doesn't give up. She figures the more she says something, the more likely someone will fall for her game. She also will use other tactics designed to "prove" how trustworthy she is. It can be extremely difficult for some unsuspecting teens to see through these words and actions to find the truth.

Secrecy

The second stage of emotional grooming is developing secrecy. Groomers persuade their targets to keep "our little secret" safe from others: *"No one, absolutely no one, can know about what we do."* This is one of the few times the groomer gives realistic reasons: *"I'll have to move away"* or *"We'll both get in trouble and not be able to see each other again."* The groomer understands that there could be real trouble if they get caught. If parents or other adults find out, the groomer and the target might face serious consequences at home. If the target is a minor and the groomer is not, the groomer could face serious legal consequences or even jail-time. That's one of the reasons the groomer works so hard to keep the relationship a secret, especially from adults.

Obviously there are different kinds of secrets. Telling your best friend about your secret crush on someone or keeping the plans for a surprise party secret are harmless secrets. But there are certain things that should never be kept secret. Anytime people talk about hurting themselves or someone else, it is your obligation to tell an adult who can help. Even if you swore you'd keep it secret, it is in everyone's best interest to tell an adult. You don't want to take the chance that this person might actually do what he or she threatens to do.

It's also wise to be suspicious of anyone who asks you to keep a secret or hide something from your parents or loved ones, especially if that secret involves your relationship. Think of it this way – when you really love someone and they really love you, you want the whole world to know. That's the nature of love – to be shared. If someone loves you and wants what's best for you, he or she isn't going to ask you to keep your relationship or anything you are doing in that relationship a secret – especially from those who love you the most.

Another way the groomer develops secrecy is by telling the target that their relationship is different from anything anyone else has ever experienced: *"No one could possibly understand how deeply we love each other. We couldn't explain it. Why spoil everything by trying to tell them how we feel?"*

Sometimes, groomers use force or threats to make sure the target won't talk: *"If anyone finds out, you'll regret it for the rest of your life"* or *"You tell anyone and you're dead meat."* Other times, the threats involve other meaningful people in the target's life: *"You don't want your little sister to accidentally get hurt now, do you?"*

The groomer often does not have to carry through on any threats. Looks, stares, glares, or other body language can keep the target under his control. Once the target fears what might happen if the secret is discovered, she will do almost anything to keep it hidden. The target is trapped. If anyone finds out, she believes she could be hurt or in trouble. She feels that the groomer holds all the power. If she wants to end the relationship and promises never to tell anyone, the groomer doesn't believe her. He continues to use whatever methods were necessary to keep the relationship a secret.

Finally, the target feels that the situation is hopeless and that she's powerless to do anything about it. She begins believing that it's better to say nothing than to risk making everything worse, and she falls deeper and deeper into secrecy. The following excerpts illustrate how groomers try to keep relationships from being discovered.

> *"We can still be secret lovers. And no one would have to know about it and it would just be our little secret. You know how much I care about you and hope you feel the same way."*

"The main thing is that you just tell me about things and don't tell no one about us. I promise you that we will have some good times. Don't let the teachers see you writing letters. Write in private! Don't worry about getting scared off by all the rules. But don't say anything to anyone, it's our secret."

"I won't do you wrong. Just trust me and no one else. Don't be goin' to no one else cause they'll only do you wrong. This is just between you and me my love."

"The feelings we have for each other are true. And will stay that way. If we start going out, we can't let others get in our way. Just remember I really do care about you in many different ways and I've fallen in love with you. You're all I want. We have to be honest with each other. And we can't tell anyone about us. You know how fast stuff spreads around here. Let's just keep it to ourselves and no one will ever need to know."

Alcohol and Drugs

Before talking about other ways the sexual con artist manipulates, it's important to understand how alcohol and drugs affect both the target and the groomer. The groomer may use drugs or alcohol as an excuse: *"I didn't know what I was doing. I was so out of it"* or *"Don't blame me, I was drunk."* Drug and alcohol use can make the sexual con artist even more aggressive and more likely to use force to get what he wants.

Drug and alcohol use also make the target easy prey for the groomer. Some teens end up involved in sexual behavior primarily because they were drunk or high. It's important to understand how drugs and alcohol affect the body.

Drug and alcohol use make it more likely that you will make poor choices or let things go too far. Being under the influence reduces your ability to make good decisions and to recognize dangerous situations. Things that may seem harmless or fun when a person is drunk or high are real problems when the person sobers up.

Here is what several surveys of young people found:

- Alcohol use by the victim, perpetrator or both has been implicated in 46 to 75 per cent of date rapes among college students.[1]

Drug or alcohol use can:

- Reduce your inhibitions.
- Impair your ability to think clearly.
- Reduce or even totally impair your ability to make good decisions.
- Delay your response time.
- Cause you to "black out" and be totally unaware of your situation.

- One survey of college students found that 78 per cent of women had experienced sexual aggression (any type of sexual activity unwanted by the woman) while on a date. Dates on which sexual aggression occurred were more likely to include heavy drinking or drug use.[2]

- 55 per cent of teens say that having sex while drinking or on drugs is often a reason for unplanned teen pregnancies.[3]

- Among 18- to 22-year-old men and women, an earlier age at initiation of alcohol use is associated with the later likelihood of having multiple sex partners.[4]

Or consider these teens' experiences:[5]

"My very best friend had a guy take advantage of her when she was drunk and she got pregnant. She doesn't know who the father is to this day. She loves her son, but how is she going to explain what happened when he gets older?"

"A few of my friends have ended up sleeping with someone after drinking that they wouldn't have otherwise slept with. Drugs and alcohol make the choice easier because you don't think of the consequences."

"Alcohol has played probably the biggest role in my decisions about sex. Of the six people I have slept with, I was drunk with four of them. "

"A friend of mine got really drunk at a party, slept with a guy she just met, and got AIDS. That one night of being intoxicated is going to cost her her life."

[1] The Centers for Disease Control and Prevention, *Youth Risk Behavior Surveillance – United States, 1999,* Morbidity and Mortality Weekly Report, June 2000, vol. 49.

[2] Ibid.

[3] The National Center of Addiction and Substance Abuse (CASA) at Columbia University, *Dangerous Liaisons: Substance Abuse and Sex,* New York, 1999.

[4] Santelli, J.S., et al., *Timing of alcohol and other drug use and sexual risk behaviors among unmarried adolescents and young adults,* Family Planning Perspectives, 2001, vol. 33.

[5] Following quotes from National Campaign to Prevent Teen Pregnancy, *Weekly Teen Survey: Sex Has Consequences,* April 18-28, 2000.

Language Cons

Language Cons are the words and phrases – or "lines" – that groomers use to trick and manipulate their targets. Language cons sometimes make a target feel special or desired; other times they make a target feel guilty or threatened. These lines may seem genuine or sincere when a target first hears them. Unfortunately, their real purpose is to control the target. Language cons are used to convince targets to do things they shouldn't do.

These words can be very seductive to an unaware teenager. Ultimately, they make targets feel powerless and helpless because they are repeated so often and are usually connected to some kind of consequence that the groomer controls. For some teens, hearing the same "line" over and over may lead to a false sense of being able to trust or depend on the groomer.

Content of Language Cons

During the early stages of emotional grooming, the groomer uses language cons to gain the target's trust and develop secrecy. The language may seem harmless at first, but these lines help the groomer gain control. As the relationship progresses, the groomer will use more sexual phrases and will make vague references to sexual contact. The groomer may start out by using words that only hint about sex: *"If I had you alone, man, you wouldn't believe how good I could make you feel."*

If the groomer meets little or no resistance to subtle sexual language cons, the content of the language cons will become more sexually graphic or even offensive and obscene. The next step may be using slang words when talking about sexual body parts or behavior. Finally, the sexual act itself is graphically described – the perpetrator uses explicit, graphic, and vulgar language to determine whether the target is receptive to the grooming process.

These lines are common language cons:

"It's okay. Don't worry."

"Just this once. Trust me."

"You know I wouldn't do anything to hurt you."

"This is normal. This is the way it's supposed to be."

"If you love me, prove it."

The groomer is "testing the water" – noting how much and what kind of sexual language the target will tolerate. If the target doesn't reject the groomer, the grooming continues. The language cons will lead into actual sexual activity. If the target does protest, the groomer may back off a little and try some other tactic. Many times, however, the groomer doesn't give up and continues the harassment.

Language cons can seem very innocent, or they may be terribly graphic. They may make a person feel good, or guilty, or threatened, or trusted. They may be sly or they may be overt. Most of the time, they are used to persuade a person into sexual activity. They always are used to control another person.

Purpose of Language Cons

Many groomers use the language of love to manipulate their targets. Groomers are aware that everyone wants to be loved, and so they do their best to convince their targets of undying love: *"I love you more each day. You're the greatest thing that ever happened to me. My love for you will last forever. I adore you."* Some targets are so hungry for love and attention that they easily fall for such lines. Most targets want to believe that someone could actually love and protect them, and they become blinded by all the attention they receive. Some targets may be having problems at home and want someone to fill the emptiness they feel.

Targets may feel really confused by everything that is happening. At times, they may feel safe and cared for. Other times, they may be a little frightened and worried. Soon, a target finds that the relationship is frequently the only thing on her mind. Even though she may know the relationship has gone too far, she feels powerless or afraid to end it. The giving and receiving of attention becomes something she likes, even though there are other parts of the relationship she doesn't like.

Even though a target may realize that what the groomer wants is wrong, she may go ahead anyway. The target has been fooled into thinking that love and sex are the same, and that it's not possible to have one without the other. If she wants to feel what she thinks is love – the groomer's attention and affection – then she must give sex. That is a distorted view of sexuality.

Sexual activity is neither a "duty" nor an "obligation." And premarital sex is no sign of loyalty and devotion to another person. Many targets also don't realize that an emotional groomer may have two or three other targets on

Language Cons can make you feel:

- **A false sense of safety or love.**
- **Frightened or worried.**
- **Obligated to be sexually active.**
- **Persuaded to run away, drink or take drugs, steal, etc.**

the line at the same time. That certainly proves he isn't "loyal" or "devoted."

Aside from convincing a target to be sexually active, the groomer often talks him or her into doing other things that may result in trouble. Running away, drinking alcohol or using drugs, stealing, or getting revenge on someone are all things that groomers may persuade their targets to do. The grooming process is usually the same – build a false sense of trust and secrecy, then manipulate the person into doing something the groomer wants.

Use of force

The more skilled and adept at emotional grooming the perpetrator is, the less he will rely on physical force. Emotional groomers rarely use physical force to coerce a person into a sexual act. This doesn't mean it hasn't happened. Instead of using physical force to get sex, most groomers rely on the relationship they have established with their targets. Most rape targets experience a trauma that is different from what targets of emotional grooming feel. Women and men who have been raped – forced in painful, violent ways to have sex against their will – see themselves as victims and readily recognize the criminal aspect of rape. These victims know they were not willing participants during their abuse.

On the other hand, most targets of emotional grooming are not aware of the criminal aspects of the grooming relationship. These targets have been convinced that they are willing participants; they may even have been convinced that they "caused" the relationship. A groomer can twist the truth to make the target think that the groomer is innocent, that nothing is wrong with the relationship, or that anything that happens is the target's fault.

When they do realize how they have been used, many targets of emotional groomers may live with guilt, humiliation, or embarrassment. The truth is that the emotional groomer is a criminal, a con artist who is just devious and shrewd enough to get away with the crime.

Emotional grooming is a process of manipulation and control. The words a groomer uses are carefully chosen. A groomer says what the target most wants to hear in order to get her to do what he wants. The language of a groomer is a con, a trick, a game. The language cons of a groomer are not just "pick-up lines." They are part of a larger plan for using another person.

Characteristics of Language Cons

The following characteristics are evident in the language of emotional groomers and players; these are the elements that set their language apart from the norm. You can use this list to analyze the language of a potential groomer.

- Trying to convince the target that sex and love are the same thing – that sexual activity is the only way to prove love

- Specific, graphic, and even offensive sexual references

- Coercive properties – using words that threaten or intimidate

- Possessiveness – treating and talking about the target like an object that is owned

- Repetitiveness – constantly using the same words to gain the target's trust

- Referring to sexual behavior as a "duty" or "responsibility"

- Referring to sexual behavior as the ultimate proof of loyalty or maturity

- Control – using words that reinforce the groomer's position as "the boss"

Even when a target tries to end the relationship, the groomer will continue to use language cons. He certainly isn't going to take the blame or admit that any type of harmful relationship ever existed. He definitely isn't going to confess that he did anything wrong. He may lie or make threats, or try to convince others that the target is crazy. Sometimes, the groomer will say that the target made everything up: *"She's always wanted me, but since I didn't pay any attention to her, she just says things to get back at me."*

It can be very difficult for a target to find the best way to stop the abuse. When targets feel powerless and afraid, they are at a loss for what to do. Some targets don't make good choices; they try to solve the problem by running away, hurting themselves, getting further involved with alcohol and drugs, or even attempting suicide. Targets who tell someone who can help, like a trusted adult or older friend, stand the best chance of getting out of the abusive situation. Many targets turn to teachers or counselors for advice.

Many groomers blame their targets for everything that happened: *"It was all your fault. You're nothing but a whore! If you hadn't wanted me so much, none of this would have ever happened."* This type of verbal abuse just adds to all of the guilt, shame, and hopelessness that the target may already feel.

The target should realize that the groomer will be just as manipulative trying to get out of the relationship as he was getting into it. Sometimes, other people won't believe what the target says at first. This is partly because the groomer used language cons with them, too. Through manipulation, he has persuaded other people to believe him. However, if the target has the courage to tell the truth, and not give up, she is on the road to recovery.

Responding to Language Cons

Some people call language cons "lines." "Lines" or language cons are thinly veiled come-on statements or outright lies used to seduce or coerce someone into sexual activity. To remember what a **line** really is, just remove the "n" – and you'll see the **lie.**

When responding to language cons, it's important to:

Remember that language cons are used to trick, manipulate, and deceive. People who use language cons are selfish and untrustworthy.

Pay close attention to a person's behaviors as well as his or her words. The old saying, "A picture is worth a thousand words," applies here. Observe how a person treats others, and listen to what he or she says to others about dating, relationships, and sex. All of these can be important indicators of an emotional groomer's hidden intentions.

Learn and practice good social skills. Developing good communication and refusal skills can help you resist giving in to threats or coercion. Build strong relationships with trustworthy adults you can go to for advice.

Don't waste time blaming yourself. There are no excuses for using another person, especially in sexual ways. People who use language cons really only want to please themselves, not others. Sexual con artists need to bear the responsibility for their words and actions. If you become a target, focus on doing things to get better rather than blaming yourself.

Be as persistent in your refusal as the person who uses language cons. He or she will use many different angles and keep trying to manipulate you. You have to be just as persistent and not give in.

Create and maintain healthy same-gender friendships. Find good friends of the same gender who have your best interests at heart. These kinds of friends can "watch your back" and help you hear and see what you may not want to notice about someone else. In other words, friends can help each other unmask a sexual con artist.

What to Say

Saying "no" to someone is difficult, especially if that person is skilled at using language cons. Some people are so "smooth" with words that you may not be able to figure out their real intentions. Therefore, it's always wise to stop and think before you agree to do something that may result in negative consequences for you.

Sexual con artists will use various kinds of lines ranging from "sweet talk" and flattery, to sexual innuendo and outright graphic sexual language. The groomer will use whatever kind of language con it takes to get what he or she wants. Sexual con artists can be very persuasive. And, convincing someone to have sex tops his or her list of priorities.

Having some idea of how you would respond can help you avoid the verbal traps set by someone who wants to convince you to have sex. You may want to use one of the following statements to help you stay in control when responding to a line.

"You don't really want me; you want sex."

"I'm not ready for sex. Don't try to push me into doing it."

"If you really care for me, you'll understand."

"Love is not sex; love is a commitment to make each other better."

"Real love isn't over in just a few minutes."

"You don't own my body. And I'm certainly not renting it out."

"Love is a two-way street. You only want it one-way: your way."

"I respect myself. Why can't you?"

"My brain's between my ears, not my legs."

"I want you to love me, not my body."

"I want real love, not an imitation."

"I have too much to lose."

"It's not worth it."

"Love is based on friendship, and you don't hurt friends."

"I want to be respected, not dejected."

"What part of 'no' don't you understand?"

"I know you don't understand, but I want you to respect my feelings."

"I care enough about you to do what's best for both of us."

"It's not right. I hope you understand."

"When I said 'no,' I meant it."

Saying 'No'

A 16-year-old girl wrote this letter to a 14-year-old boy who was frequently writing her notes. Notice the various ways in which she said "no."

"Hello. I am going to be very blunt and honest with you. NO. I do not like you at all and I have no interest in getting to know you whatsoever. First of all, you are younger than me and I am looking for different qualities in a guy than what you have. No, there's nothing wrong with you but I want someone different and maturity is a main quality. Please quit writing me notes. No, I'm not going to give you a chance. Yes, you are wasting your time. Sorry, but I'm a blunt person. Lay off. Sorry if I broke your heart. Very uninterested and sorry."

The Nine
Grooming Tactics

So how do you learn how to recognize a groomer? Learning what emotional grooming is, the elements of the grooming process, and the language cons used by groomers are all helpful tools you can learn to help better recognize a sexual con artist. Groomers can also be identified by the specific tactics they use to manipulate others. Once you can recognize these nine grooming tactics as manipulative and unhealthy behaviors, you can more easily detect and avoid the "playas" altogether.

Normal or Harmful?

Please note that some of these tactics, outside of an emotional grooming relationship, are normal feelings. These normal feelings only become grooming tactics when that feeling is used to manipulate someone else. Then it becomes a harmful and wrong use of that emotion. Jealousy, insecurity, and anger are all normal human emotions, but when used to manipulate or control someone else, they become grooming tactics.

Take jealousy, for example. Even though it's not a happy feeling, it is common and most people have felt jealous at one time or another. Imagine that you see your boyfriend standing very close to and talking with a very attractive classmate. Perhaps you feel jealous. That would be normal. However, it is how you act on that jealousy that makes your reaction harmful or healthy. If you beat up the other girl, threaten to hurt yourself, or try to damage your boyfriend's car, you are acting in a way that is meant to manipulate your boyfriend into paying full attention to you. That's emotional grooming.

So how do you handle feeling jealous (or angry or insecure) without resorting to grooming? Learn to simply name, claim, and tame the feeling. Specifically, name and admit that you're feeling jealous, tell your boyfriend or a trusted adult how you feel. Together find a constructive way to deal with the situation, and then let it go. That's a healthy response to a tough feeling.

Most of the nine grooming tactics are **always** manipulative and **always** unhealthy in any relationship. Take, for example, the grooming tactics of bribery and intimidation. No matter what, intimidation and bribery should never happen in a healthy relationship. You should never hang around or date someone who threatens, intimidates, or tries to bribe you. Nothing good will come of a relationship like that.

The nine grooming tactics are:

1. Jealousy and possessiveness
2. Insecurity
3. Intimidation
4. Anger
5. Accusations
6. Flattery
7. Status
8. Bribery
9. Control

In the next section, you'll read excerpts from notes and letters written by and to teens. Each excerpt illustrates the tactics groomers use to manipulate and control others. Read on to find out more about each of the nine grooming tactics.

Jealousy and Possessiveness

As mentioned earlier, jealousy is a normal, albeit difficult human emotion. Jealousy only becomes a grooming tactic when it is used to control or manipulate someone else. Acting out in a jealous rage, spreading vicious rumors, attempting to emotionally or physically hurt someone you are jealous of, or using jealousy to manipulate someone – those are examples of emotional grooming.

A groomer may express his jealousy through possessive and controlling words and behaviors. The groomer doesn't want anyone else "messing" with his "territory." This may include attempting to control who the target can talk to, hang out with, how she can dress, or even how she spends money. The groomer acts as if he completely owns his target's feelings and behaviors and is resentful and extremely jealous of anyone who gets any kind of attention from his "possession."

> *"I'm telling you now and one time only, I want his stuff out of your locker. What kind of fool do I look like? I'm going out with you, but your ex-boyfriend is still in your locker. No! That is not going to happen. I want his stuff out. Today! If you're my girl his stuff has to go."*

Treating someone like an object to own rather than a person to relate to is at the heart of jealousy and possessiveness. You may see and hear signs of this everywhere: *"She's my woman," "You can't talk to him," "You belong to me,"* and so on. But remember, people are not objects to be owned or possessed or controlled.

There's another way a groomer might use jealousy to control her target. She may attempt to make the target feel jealous in order to get him to "prove" his love. She may say or do things to provoke feelings of jealousy and possessiveness.

"I want us to be together for the rest of your days here but I do need some type of "social" life with boys, cuz baby you ain't giving none up."

Using jealousy to control or "own" someone else or trying to provoke feelings of jealousy in someone else are both grooming tactics. Both are signs that a relationship is off to an unhealthy start.

But everyone feels jealous some time or another, right? True! The key to healthy relationships lies in learning how to handle jealousy, and all our other feelings, appropriately. One method of handling emotions appropriately is to **name, claim** and **tame** your feelings.

Name – Spend some time figuring out what it is you are feeling. Often we just react to negative or difficult feelings without really being aware of the actual emotion. It is helpful to name your feeling, so that you can move beyond it.

Claim – To claim your feeling means to own it. *"I feel jealous"* is different from *"You make me so jealous."* Using "I" language helps you to recognize the feeling as your own, rather than blaming it on others.

Tame – To tame a feeling means to find a way to express it appropriately, without hurting yourself or someone else. Usually this means finding a trusted adult or wise friend who will enable you to name and claim your feelings, encourage you to find ways to express feelings appropriately (like writing in a journal, talking it out, crying, counseling, etc.), and finally who will support you in accepting and letting go of the emotion. Taming ultimately involves recognizing and accepting what you can and cannot control in life. It's not an easy process, but it will help you to grow and to have happier and healthier relationships.

Insecurity

Like jealousy, insecurity is a normal human emotion. In some cases, it's even appropriate to feel somewhat insecure. And like jealousy, insecurity is a grooming tactic **only** when it is used to manipulate someone else.

The groomer uses insecurity to manipulate in two ways. One way the groomer misuses insecurity is to act insecure and ask for constant reassurance of the target's love and loyalty. The target is expected to take care of this insecurity by writing love letters or telling the groomer how great she is and how much she is loved. She also may want pity and sympathy – someone to feel sorry for her.

> *"I guess it's no big deal. I just don't think I'm really your type or good enough for you. I'm screwing too many things up. I'm not worth it. So let me know if you want to stop our relationship, I'll try to understand. I probably deserve it anyway. The way I treat you, I'm not doing it the way I'm supposed to. I guess I was wrong. I'm sorry for treating you the way I did."*

The groomer may take insecurity so far as to say something like *"I'll kill myself if you leave me!"* Use great caution if you hear this statement. It may just be an idle threat, a ploy used to get you to stay in the relationship. But we never know for sure what someone else's true intentions are. If you ever hear someone threatening suicide or to hurt you or someone else, you must tell an adult – a parent, a teacher, a counselor, a police officer, or a pastor.

It is never your obligation to stay in a relationship with a person who is threatening to hurt himself or herself, but it is your obligation to tell an adult who can help. Threats of self-harm can sometimes turn into harm acted out against others. Criminal justice advocate Laura Delgado says it this way, "A threat of suicide is exactly the same as a threat of homicide ...It says that 'I don't have anything to lose.'"

The other misuse of insecurity is when the groomer attempts to magnify the target's insecurities or create new insecurities.

"No one else will ever want you. I'm the only one who is ever going to want you. You'd be stupid to pass up a guy like me. I'm the man. Once I'm through with you, you'll never want anybody else."

This kind of manipulation is an attempt to control the target's thoughts and feelings about herself. The groomer hopes that the target will feel so bad and so insecure about herself that she will stay in a relationship with the groomer and become more reluctant to open up to others.

Intimidation

Intimidation is a powerful form of manipulation. Unlike jealousy or insecurity, intimidation is not a normal human emotion, and has no place in healthy relationships.

The groomer intimidates by frightening, coercing, or threatening others into submission. The intimidation can be verbal, nonverbal, or a combination of both. Some groomers are quite skilled at intimidating, and getting what they want from others, with just a glance or a gesture. Intimidation is always wrong and is always manipulative.

One type of verbal intimidation is threatening. For example, a groomer may threaten to hurt the target or someone close to the target, threaten to take a favorite possession of the target and damage or destroy it as a warning of what could happen, or threaten to "tell on" something the target has done wrong.

Verbal intimidation is used to make the target feel uncomfortable and uneasy and the groomer to feel in control. Groomers use intimidating and threatening language to "test the waters" and see how much a target will tolerate. These verbal scare tactics often work; the target becomes too afraid to say "no" and may even worry about her safety.

> *"I'm not mad at you, as long as you're not lying to me. If I find out you are lying, you and me are finished. So, if you're not telling me something, you better spill it now. I don't want to have to find out later from someone else. I can find out!"*

> *"I'm sure I confused the s--- out of you. One minute I'm mean to you, the next minute I'm whispering I love you while tapping your chest with my water bottle. It was all a play for the girls."*

Another form of verbal intimidation is when the groomer uses sexually explicit and/or offensive language when speaking to the target. The groomer may:

- Use vulgar sexual language in front of the target.

- Make sexual noises or sounds (catcalls, howling, barking, etc.).

- Use specific, graphic sexual descriptions of what the groomer wants to do to the target.

- Ask questions that are too personal or sexual in nature.

The groomer uses graphic or offensive sexual language for various reasons:

- To scare the target into participating in the described sexual behavior

- To desensitize the target so that he or she will become used to this kind of language and eventually this kind of sexual behavior

- To test the target's limits and boundaries – if the target laughs, giggles, or even just ignores sexually explicit or obscene language, it gives the groomer the "green light" to continue pushing for sexual activity

- To sexually arouse the target

You do not have to tolerate, listen to or participate in sexually explicit, obscene or offensive language. It's best to just walk away from language like this. Better yet, if this kind of talk is taking place in or at school functions, tell a teacher or administrator. Often this kind of language can be a form of sexual harassment – and sexual harassment is illegal! Help your teachers and administrators help you by reporting sexually explicit, offensive or vulgar notes, pictures, e-mails, or language!

Often the groomer will use threatening words in conjunction with intimidating physical actions – looming over someone who is seated, standing too close, touching or grabbing others, using loud and controlling voice tones and language, staring at sexual body parts, hitting the palm of the hand real hard, snapping a pencil in two, or faking a punch. Male groomers may take intimidating stances when girls walk by – slouching over, holding their hands on their crotches, howling, whistling, or making catcalls.

Remember, sexually graphic, offensive, or vulgar gestures can also be forms of sexual harassment. You don't have to tolerate it. But do report it!

Anger

Like jealousy, anger is a normal human emotion. In some circumstances, anger can even be justifiable and produce positive change. But none of this is true when a groomer uses anger to manipulate.

For the groomer, angry outbursts are a way to control and get what he or she wants from others. Unfortunately, using explosive anger to get what you want is depicted and often glorified in many types of contemporary media – from TV talk shows and action films to music videos. And all too often adults do not model appropriate ways of expressing and managing angry feelings. The result is that many teens lack the modeling and social skills necessary for proper anger management.

More and more teens are misusing anger in dating relationships or allowing themselves to get hurt by others' uncontrolled anger. Teen dating violence is on the rise. Consider these statistics:

- One in every five high school girls has been physically or sexually abused by a dating partner.[1]

- A disturbing number of boys have adopted attitudes that men are entitled to control their girlfriends through violence.[2]

- A 1999 Massachusetts survey of students reported that 16 per cent of girls and 6 per cent of boys have had sexual contact against their will.[3]

A groomer's anger can be displayed in a variety of ways – yelling, screaming, hitting, or throwing things. Regardless of how it is expressed, the groomer's explosive anger is used to threaten, intimidate and manipulate others. And whenever anger is used to manipulate and hurt others, it's wrong.

Because he usually gets what he wants from others when he misuses anger in this way, the groomer will use angry outbursts to threaten or intimidate his target into some kind of sexual act. Since the target doesn't want to lose her boyfriend or may be afraid that he will take his anger out on her, she engages in the sexual behavior.

"So, he called you? What was his name? I know you at least know that. I've told you not to mess with me! People get hurt when they mess with me. Unless I find out your lying to me. If I find out you are, be ready, because I'm going off. That's why I said if you left something out, tell me now."

An emotional groomer who uses anger to manipulate and intimidate others can be very dangerous. His outbursts may happen more frequently or become more violent. He may even connect sex with the power his angry outbursts have given him. After a while, he may believe that sex is good only when force or pain is involved.

"Today I seen Antwan when I was outside with everyone. He came up there and snatched me up then beat my a--. I

fought back, I don't care who he is. Then after a while, my stomach started hurting and I threw up. Later I was laying on his lap and he said he was sorry and we ended up doin' the nasty."

Even some of the language used to describe the sex act is violent. Some groomers describe sex with phrases like "knocking boots," "Let's hit it," "I'm gonna get me a piece of that," "Tag that a--," or "thumping." Words like "tag," "hit," "knock," or "thump" reveal the groomer's true intent – to hurt and use another person. Referring to the other person as an object – "piece of that," "it," or "bones" – enables the groomer to distance himself from the target and makes it easier to use another person.

Some forms of contemporary media, especially music and music videos, contribute to this connection between sex and violence. Lyrics of many contemporary songs contain violent references to sexual activity. The numerous repetitions of such violent sexual imagery only serve to make it seem more "normal" or acceptable and end up desensitizing listeners or viewers to its aggressive and unhealthy nature.

Herein lies the problem: If you think and talk about sex in violent and aggressive terms, (and many teens and adults

> ## Chain Reaction of Thoughts
>
> Examine and screen your thoughts
>
> Because your thoughts become your words
>
> Your words become your actions
>
> Your actions become your habits
>
> Your habits become your character
>
> And your character becomes your destiny
>
> – ANONYMOUS

do use these terms when "joking" around or singing along with favorite songs), then it follows that sooner or later you will act on sex in this manner – being violent or aggressive in a sexual relationship or allowing someone to mistreat you in this way. It's like a "chain reaction," the way you talk about something influences the way you think about something, and that in turn will influence the way you behave.

Accusations

When using this tactic, the groomer creates false or exaggerated accusations to frighten, threaten and ultimately control the target. For example, a groomer might accuse his girlfriend of having sex with other guys or talking about him behind his back. Regardless of the specifics of the accusation, the real intent is to publicly intimidate and perhaps even humiliate the target, thus maximizing the groomer's sense of control.

> *"Just tell me or not if you did anything with Booker. If you want him, just go out with him. I'll get over it. It's not like you would really care anyway. He even came up to me and said some things about you and him, and what you did. Don't do this to me, even when I hear this stuff, it hurts my feelings. I wouldn't be surprised if you're playing on me."*

Flattery

Most emotional groomers are "smooth talkers." They know what to say and how to say it so that they impress others and appear completely trustworthy. A groomer uses language cons that lure the target into thinking she is the most important person in his world, and that he's the best guy for her. The groomer does not give sincere or honest compliments. He merely uses flattery – exaggerated and insincere comments – to get what he wants. Sometimes, the flattery may be appropriate, but it usually is sexually suggestive or graphic. Even though the groomer's flattery may be insincere and manipulative, the target may still enjoy the attention.

> *"I wanted to say 'I like you' when I first saw you. You made me feel special. Lucky is the guy who gets to be with a diamond like you, your eyes are so beautiful your body your hair, everything. You are like candy, once a guy gets a taste of you he will go crazy."*

> *"I know a lot of guys like me, but I don't like them. You seem like a nice person to me. I hope that one day you and I will be closer together. You look good and you know it."*

We all like to hear nice things said about us. But it's important to know the difference between flattery and sincere compliments. With flattery there's always a string attached, something wanted or expected in return. Compliments are different. Compliments are given to make the other person feel good – with no strings attached.

A sincere and genuine compliment shows approval or admiration for people or for their accomplishments. It is specific and truthful. Learning how to give and how to accept compliments are important relationship-building skills. When complimenting others, rather than focusing on a person's looks, try paying attention to and complimenting what others have accomplished or who they are on the inside, their personal qualities. Giving sincere compliments that recognize a person's talents and accomplishments is a sure way to get a relationship started in the right direction.

Status

Sometimes, others "look up to" the groomer. He could be a good athlete; she might have a lot of money; he may have access to alcohol or drugs, or she may be the most popular or most attractive girl at school. Whatever the reason for the status, the groomer uses his or her popularity to lure a target into a sexual relationship. More often than not, the target likes hanging around with someone with so much status and popularity and will often be convinced that sex is "owed" to the emotional groomer because of the attention, popularity, or favors the groomer's status gives the target.

> "I do like you a lot even though we're not going out. If I didn't would I waste 5 minutes of a phone call on you? Would I call you when there's a lot more girls that I could be calling or would I even talk to you? I'm not too good for you at all because there's no such thing. Please believe me I do care and like you and I wouldn't be wasting my time if I didn't."

> "I understand that you want a fine babe like me, so don't get all choked up. You treat me right and you'll see what that brings you."

For some, having sex also can be a way to gain status. Some teens think having sex will prove they are "macho," "cool" or "grown up." Other teens think dating someone several years older will give him or her a certain status among friends. Both of these kinds of teens are vulnerable to emotional groomers.

Bribery

Bribery is "giving to get." The groomer may give material things to his target, but these "gifts" always have a string attached. In healthy relationships, giving gifts can be a normal sign of friendship or love. In an unhealthy relationship, a groomer gives "gifts" in order to bribe or manipulate the target. The target may think that something, usually some sort of sexual behavior, must be done to "pay back" the groomer so that the attention and gifts will continue.

Sometimes, the bribe that convinces a target to stay with a groomer may be the promise of marriage or of always being together. Female groomers will often use the promise of sex as a bribe to get and keep a guy in a relationship. In some relationships, the bribes are alcohol or drugs. This is an old trick used by pimps with their prostitutes: Get them addicted to a substance and they will do whatever the pimp wants.

"If I could do it I'd buy you everything you wanted. Remember that sweater at the mall. That would look so good on you baby. Someday I'll buy it or steal it if I have to. You mean the world to me and I want to show you how much. You just keep being good to me, you'll see."

Bribery can sometimes be very blatant and very destructive. A 16-year-old girl told her teacher: *"When I was 13, my boyfriend, who was 19, took me to the fair. He won one of those big stuffed teddy bears. When we got home he told me he'd give me the bear if I had sex with him. How come when he was on top of me, I started crying?"* The teacher responded, *"You cried because he was taking something precious from you that you weren't ready to give. That's where the tears came from."* It's obvious that this groomer used bribery to get what he wanted. He gave a 13-year-old girl a toy in order to get sex from her.

Unfortunately, this attitude of "giving to get" appears to be widespread among many boys and men in our society. According to a recent survey, 30 per cent of seventh to ninth grade boys believed that a girl owes them sex if they spend a lot of money on her. Even more frightening is the attitude that it is acceptable to force sex on a girl if necessary. This type of thinking is devastating to the moral, sexual, and social development of young people.

Control

The ultimate goal of an emotional groomer is to gain control of the target and of the relationship. The groomer wants to control not only what his target does, but also how he or she thinks and feels. The groomer seeks to gain power or dominance in the relationship by using any or all of the grooming tactics described. Remember, some groomers are "playing" this game of control and manipulation with two or three other targets at the same time. If a particular tactic won't work with one target, the groomer will try it with another target.

> *"If you get in trouble doing anything wrong and I hear about it, you will deal with me. I don't want to do anything with any other girl except you. I'm the only one who is right for you. So don't play on me, OK. You wouldn't want to see me mad. Just do what I say. If you're smart you'll listen good."*

> *"I really do love you baby and I don't want you to feel like your being pressured into this relationship. But you gotta know that I'm the man. I want you to be positive about this relationship. I don't want you to have the impression that if you see me talking to another girl that I'm playing you. I want to be true and I want you to think I'm being true to this relationship. Yo baby I want this relationship to work out. I won't do you wrong. Just trust me."*

Someone is too controlling if he or she:

- Calls constantly to check up on you.

- Tells you how to dress, who to hang out with, how to spend your time or money.

- Forces or manipulates you into doing what he or she wants.

- Sends harassing or threatening e-mails, messages, or notes.

- Physically, emotionally, or sexually abuses you.

- Uses violence or intimidation to get his or her way.

- Humiliates or puts you down in public.

- Makes demands or gives orders.

- Tries to get you to keep the relationship a secret.

- Has an explosive temper – throws objects, slams doors, punches walls, etc.

- Refuses to listen to or show respect to you and others.

- Attempts to keep you away from friends or family.

- Gives gifts to get something from you in return.

- Spreads rumors about you.

- Threatens suicide or self-harm.

Results of Being Groomed

The following letter expresses how a young woman felt about being groomed.

"How ya doing? I'm doing ok, but not the best. I have some things I kinda need to get off my chest and I need to do it now! OK! You were a great friend before everything happened. I loved being around you and enjoyed you as a person! I always had a crush on you and always wanted us to become closer.

"Then you started talking to Heather more. And I had class with you so that gave me the chance to get to know you and I jumped on it! I felt very good about how our relationship was going. But something inside wanted to get to know you better! A.J. told me you had some kind of feelings or something like that and I became more 'wanting something.' I don't know how to say it.

"Then there was that night! That night I enjoyed very much! I haven't had those feelings in a long time! But, those feelings got mixed up somewhere. I knew nothen was gonna happen with us. So, I wasn't waiting for you to come up and ask me out! But, well, I don't know what I expected.

"OK, I'm going to put this as clear as I can! What I did that night was something special. I don't do that with just any guy. I felt that everything was ok. But then when I got back and the first thing I hear about is Heather and you did what, I felt nasty! I heard what you said I did and I didn't know what to do. I felt like a pile of s---. I guess I felt used in a way. My two weeks have been hell!! I couldn't hold anything

down, I got depressed all the time, I was scared to go to school, and I feel like I lost a great friend because of all this! Sometimes I wish none of this ever happened to me. I have been hurt by too many guys. I don't feel right around you! I feel like I was used for a free night and then forgot about. Left in the dust for the next person to come along. I feel sick! I can't even face you as myself anymore because I feel so bad!"

Her words speak volumes of the hurt caused by grooming. If you analyze her letter closely, you'll notice the groomer used various tactics to manipulate her into a sexual encounter. He successfully developed a false sense of trust and then attempted to make her feel jealous and insecure by making sure that she noticed him talking to and spending time with other girls. For this young woman, and many other guys and girls like her, the results were emotionally devastating.

[1] Journal of American Medical Association, August 2001.
[2] Ibid.
[3] Massachusetts Dept. of Education, 1999, www.doe.mass.edu.

5

Boundaries

Teens Can become less vulnerable to emotional grooming by learning how to set healthy boundaries for themselves and to respect others' boundaries as well. This chapter defines what healthy boundaries are, teaches you how to set and maintain appropriate boundaries, and gives suggestions on how to spot boundary problems in yourself and others.

What Are Boundaries?

There's a certain healthy physical and emotional distance that you keep between yourself and others. This distance is often referred to as your "boundaries." Boundaries are the limits you have set for relationships. Boundaries define where you end and where someone else begins. They help you to recognize what is and what is **not** your responsibility in relationships.

Imagine a series of invisible circles around your physical and emotional self. These circles determine how close you will let people get to you. These circles represent the various kinds of boundaries we all have. Boundaries help you determine how much you will share with others and how open or emotionally and physically close you will be with all the various people in your life.

Boundaries work in two ways – they let people in, and they keep people out. Boundaries protect your thoughts, feelings, body, and behavior. They help tell you what's right and wrong. Setting and maintaining healthy boundaries can help you to protect yourself, take responsibility for yourself, and can even help you gain respect and show respect for others.

There are two types of boundaries:

External – External boundaries protect your body, keeping it safe and healthy. External boundaries have two components – physical and sexual. Physical boundaries protect your body, and sexual boundaries protect your sexual body parts and your sexuality.

Internal – Internal boundaries protect your thoughts and emotions. Internal boundaries have two components – emotional and spiritual. Emotional boundaries help you protect your feelings, and spiritual boundaries help you protect the deepest part of who you are – your sense of hope, trust, mystery, security, and sense of spirituality.

Learning About Boundaries

You begin learning about and setting boundaries at an early age. Your parents help teach you right from wrong, as well as how and who to be physically and emotionally close with. When you were young, your parents probably had all kinds of rules for you, like "Look both ways before crossing the street" or "Don't talk to strangers." Both of these rules are also boundaries, designed to help you protect your physical, emotional, sexual, and spiritual self.

As you grow older and begin to develop more and more relationships outside your family, you begin to put what you've learned about boundaries into practice. Think about emotional boundaries for a moment. In your family, you probably learned to trust your parents and siblings enough to tell them your personal thoughts and feelings. As we grow older, most people continue to share their private thoughts and feelings only with family and best friends.

People with healthy boundaries are selective about whom they allow inside their closest emotional and physical boundaries. They know that most relationships, like those with casual acquaintances or classmates, are not as personal and therefore it would not be wise to share personal thoughts, feelings, or experiences within such relationships. Not enough trust has been established. Casual acquaintances should talk about "light" and non-personal topics like the weather, sports, movies, schoolwork, or current events.

People with healthy boundaries would also never consider telling strangers about personal information. They learned long ago that "Don't talk to strangers" was a good boundary designed to protect them. As a teen or young adult, you may occasionally talk to strangers, but only about the time, sports, weather or directions – never about anything personal.

As an example of physical boundaries, think about riding in an elevator alone. You have all that space to yourself, and you can move around as you please. Gradually, other people get on the elevator. You're not as comfortable as when you were alone. More people get on the elevator; someone steps on your foot, you feel scrunched in a corner. You smell someone's breath and body odor. You feel uneasy because other people have entered the space where you once felt comfortable. They are just too close. You feel crowded and uneasy. They have crossed your physical boundaries.

For most Americans, a comfortable physical boundary with strangers is having an arm's length distance from that person. In other countries or cultures, the physical distance, or comfort zone, with strangers may be different.

Physical boundaries, or comfort zones, change depending on the relationship and may also change over time as the relationship changes. Think about going on a first date. This person is a casual acquaintance. You probably would not feel comfortable holding hands yet. But after several dates, you may trust the other person enough to hold hands, slow dance, or even hug.

Boundary Crossing

In the elevator example, the people were strangers. Had they been your friends, you may not have felt as uncomfortable. But the same uncomfortable feeling of having your boundaries "crossed" **can** occur in friendships and other close relationships, too. Friends and even family members can violate your boundaries. When friends or family violate your trust, they also violate your boundaries.

Some boundary violations include:

■ Interrupting a conversation

People with healthy boundaries:

- **Are secure about themselves.**

- **Don't let others intrude.**

- **Have a clear sense of their own views, values, and priorities.**

- **Are confident.**

- **Can protect themselves without shutting off from others.**

- **Know how to stand up for themselves at appropriate times.**

- **Are able to enter into relationships without losing their own identity.**

- **Are able to identify safe and appropriate people.**

- Taking one of your possessions without permission

- Teasing or making fun of you

- Asking very personal questions

- Gossiping about others

- Touching your body without your permission

- Telling other people stories about you

- Telling other people private information about you

- Always being around you – making you feel uncomfortable by invading your "private space"

- Using offensive, vulgar, or sexually explicit language in your presence

- Forcing you into doing something sexual

- Physically abusing you

So what should you do when someone crosses or violates your boundaries? Think of a soccer or basketball game. What happens when the ball goes out of bounds? The game stops for a few minutes. The team and the coaches may even meet to decide what to do next.

It's a lot like that in life, too. When someone crosses one of your boundaries, whether it is a stranger, friend, or family member, you need to step back from the situation and decide what to do next. It may help to talk to someone else you trust about what happened. Describe the situation, as well as how you feel. Ask for help deciding what to do next. In most cases, it's important to tell the person who violated your boundary what he or she did and how it was hurtful to you.

Usually, an apology from the boundary crosser can go a long way toward rebuilding trust and the relationship. But remember, some boundary violations are serious enough that you should never let that person emotionally, physically, sexually, or spiritually close to you again.

Boundary Problems

Appropriate boundaries protect a person's physical, sexual, emotional, and spiritual self. But when appropriate boundaries aren't set, it can create a dangerous situation where you could get hurt or end up hurting someone else.

There are two kinds of boundary problems. Boundaries can be too open (indiscriminately sharing private thoughts, feelings or experiences with others you don't know well) or boundaries can be too closed (never sharing personal thoughts and emotions with others). Here are some signs of each kind of boundary problem.

Your boundaries are too open if you:

- Can't say "no."

- Share too much personal information.

- Take responsibility for others' feelings.

- Allow yourself to be abused.

- Reveal personal thoughts, feelings, or experiences to acquaintances or strangers.

- Believe you deserve bad treatment.

- Can't see flaws in others.

- Will do anything to avoid conflict.

- Engage in public displays of affection.

- Wear revealing or seductive clothing (including sagging pants).

- Stand or sit too close to others.

- Make sexual comments, jokes, or noises in public.

- Trust strangers.

- Believe everything you hear.

- Have sexual encounters with acquaintances or strangers.

Your boundaries are too closed if you:

- Always say "no" to requests that might require you to get close to somebody.

- Share little or nothing about yourself.

- Are unable to identify your own wants, needs, and feelings.

- Don't have any friends.

- Don't let adults help.

- Never ask for help, even when needed.

- Refuse to let trustworthy adults touch you appropriately (handshakes, pats on the back).

A Boundary Questionnaire

How do you know if a relationship has unhealthy boundaries? A careful reading and discussion of the topics in this book should give you a pretty good idea of what an unhealthy relationship looks like and sounds like. You should be better at recognizing the nine grooming tactics and the emotional grooming process. The following questions can help you take a closer look at your friendships and dating relationships. Be honest with yourself as you answer these questions. These questions may help point out unhealthy qualities in some of your relationships.

1. Does this person try to tell me what to do, how to dress, whom to hang out with?

2. Do I spend most of my time worrying about this relationship?

3. Does it seem that this person purposefully tries to make me feel jealous or insecure?

4. Does it seem that I do all the giving and my friend does all the taking?

5. Does my friend put unrealistic demands on me? What demands?

6. Does my friend ignore me or attempt to control me when others are around? What usually happens?

7. Does it seem like this friend is always trying to change me? How?

8. Does my friend purposefully do things to hurt me emotionally or physically? What?

9. Do other people tell me that my friend talks behind my back? About what?

10. Do I get into trouble when I do what my friend says? How?

11. Do I feel ashamed, guilty, or afraid after talking or being with this person?

12. Have I quit doing things that I used to enjoy since I've become involved with this person? What? Why?

13. Does this person ever threaten or intimidate me?

14. Has this person ever given me a gift and expected sexual contact in return?

A "yes" to any of these questions points to an unhealthy characteristic in your friendship. The more "yes" answers you gave, the more unhealthy qualities your friendship has. Take some time to figure out if you can correct what's going wrong (or if the friendship is worth it). On the other hand, a lot of "no" answers indicate that you and your friend have a good friendship. See what you can do to make it even better.

What to Do

If you feel you've been used or abused in a relationship, there are a number of steps you can take:

Tell someone who can help. Talk to someone you trust – a parent, a professional counselor, teacher, or other adult who will listen and offer help.

Understand that change is possible. You're not weird or crazy. What happened was not your fault; someone took advantage of you. It's time to begin a new life that's free from abuse.

Be honest. Admit that something bad happened to you. Don't make excuses for yourself or the person who used you. Don't hide the secret anymore. The pain will never stop if you don't do something about it. Let the pain end so the healing can begin.

Call the toll-free Girls and Boys Town National Hotline at 1-800-448-3000. Counselors are on call day and night to help with any problem.

Name, claim and tame your feelings. You may be fearful, anxious, depressed or just plain angry. All these feelings are normal. Name what you're feeling; expect some strong emotions. But don't keep your feelings bottled up inside. Talk to your counselor. Ask for ideas on how to handle feelings appropriately. Read books on how to handle negative or strong emotions. If you're depressed, ask for help; if you're angry, learn how to manage your anger, etc. Don't just feel badly; do something about it!

> **Try the P-O-P method of solving problems:**
>
> **P** – Identify the problem situation.
>
> **O** – List various options for handling the situation and the advantages and disadvantages of each.
>
> **P** – Decide on a plan to handle the problem by choosing one of the options to put into action. Assess the success of your plan and decide if anything else needs to be done.

Learn to recognize the kinds of people and situations that can get you in trouble. Do some problem solving to find ways to avoid or get away from abusive people and negative environments.

Learn how to create and maintain healthy boundaries. Read all you can about healthy boundaries and friendship. Observe people who have good boundaries and healthy friendships. Take notice of what makes good relationships grow. Then put into practice what you've learned.

Learn healthy responses to stress. Things may worry you; people may upset you. Get involved in positive activities. Join a support group. Exercise. Doing kind and helpful things for others will help you avoid getting bogged down in self-pity.

Setting Appropriate Boundaries

There are many ways to set and maintain appropriate boundaries. The following tips can help you set good boundaries:

- Identify teens and adults you can trust and build relationships with them.

- Avoid people who are selfish, disrespectful, manipulative or abusive. Such people will likely disrespect you and your boundaries.

- Spend time with people who do well in school and at home, who are liked and respected by many people. Such people are more likely to have good boundaries themselves and will be more likely to respect your boundaries too.

- Learn to say "no" when you're being pressured to do something wrong. Anyone who pressures or invites you to do something wrong doesn't respect you or your boundaries.

- Trust your sense of safety or danger. These are good indicators of right and wrong. If someone or something seems dangerous or threatening, stay away!

- Learn how to think through and solve problems before reacting. Problem solving and critical thinking skills can help you maintain your boundaries and respect others.

- Think about times when your personal boundaries were violated. Who was involved? What was the situation? Think of a better way to handle boundary violations in the future.

- Speak up when someone or something bothers you. Talk to adults you can trust.

- Set limits about where you will go, what you will do, and how long you will be there. Having and sticking to a plan helps you keep and respect boundaries.

- Find ways to tell (or show) others what your personal boundaries are.

Rules for Good Boundaries

Different kinds of relationships have different kinds of boundaries. Your physical, emotional, sexual, and spiritual boundaries with your parents and siblings are different than the boundaries you have with friends. The boundaries you set with a stranger should be different than the boundaries you have with classmates or co-workers.

Below are some good points to consider as a relationship or friendship is developing. These are general rules you can follow that can help you establish and maintain good boundaries in all your relationships. Honestly reflecting on each of these areas can help you make wise decisions about who you decide to become friends with or to date.

Length of time – How long have you known this person? How can knowing someone longer be beneficial to you? How long is long enough before a stranger becomes a friend? How do you decide?

Knowledge about the other person – What, and how much, do you really know about this person? Some important things to know about someone you are considering dating are:

- How does this person react when given "no" for an answer?

- How does this person handle frustrations and disappointments?

- How does he or she express anger?

- How does this person treat his or her parents?

- How does this person speak about and treat the other gender?

How can this knowledge help you make good choices in a relationship? Explain or give examples.

Sharing activities – How many different kinds of activities have you shared together? What are they? How have these experiences helped you get to know the other person better?

Amount of self-disclosure – How much personal information have you shared? How much has the other person shared? Are you comfortable with the sharing? Why or why not? Is the amount of sharing equal between the two of you?

Number of different experiences – What has this person experienced in life? How has it affected him or her? What can this person's experiences tell you about him or her?

Role appropriate – We all have certain roles in life. Some roles are not compatible for dating or friendship relationships. Teachers shouldn't date students; doctors should not date patients, etc. What role does this person have in your life?

Age appropriate – As a teen, friendships or dating relationships with those more than two years older or younger than you can be harmful. What is the age difference between you? If it is greater than two years, how could this be harmful?

Level of reciprocal trust – Can you trust this person? How do you know? Are you worthy of his or her trust? Why? How do you know when someone is trustworthy? What happens when trust is broken?

Explaining the Rules

Length of Time

When developing a new relationship, remember that time is on your side! Really getting to know someone takes time. It doesn't happen overnight. The more you know about someone, the better judgments you can make about how close to allow him or her. Never rush into a relationship or allow someone to rush you. Take it gradually. If it is good and healthy boundaries are respected, it will last.

Knowledge about the Other Person

Getting to know someone involves spending "real" time together, (not just "virtual time" chatting on the computer), as well as talking about many things – his or her family, likes and dislikes, hopes and dreams for the future, past experiences, etc. If you are considering a close relationship with someone, there are some really important things you should know about including: How does this person react when hearing "no" for an answer? How does he or she treat brothers, sisters, and parents? How does he or she speak about the opposite gender when with friends? How does this person handle frustrations and anger?

You can learn such important information not only by discussing these issues but also by observing how he or she interacts with others. This is why group dating can be helpful. It allows you to see the other person interact with a variety of people. If he or she is a player, they won't be able to hide it for long. Remember, the more you know, the better your decisions can be.

Amount of Self-Disclosure and Trust

How much personal information should you share with someone you are just getting to know? The best rule of thumb is to share a small bit of personal information, something you wouldn't really mind if others found out about. Then see what happens. If he or she respects you and your boundaries, then your personal information won't become public news. But if he or she does share your personal information with others, it's a sure sign that this person is not trustworthy.

How do you know if someone is really trustworthy? Remember that real trust is built. It takes time. It is something we prove through our actions, not just something we say with words. A trustworthy person is someone who keeps his or her promises, who is there for you in good times and in bad, and who tells you the truth even when it's hard.

Trust is hard earned but easily broken. Sometimes even our family and closest friends will break our trust and violate our boundaries. When that happens, an apology with appropriate amends can go a long way toward rebuilding trust and repairing the relationship.

Role and Age Appropriate

We all have certain roles in life. Some roles are incompatible for dating relationships or even friendship. Teachers should not date or seek students out as friends. Doctors should not date patients. Coaches should not date or seek out the athletes they coach as friends. Certain relationships are designed to be dependent, where one person has more knowledge, power, or status than the other. Because of their dependent nature, these types of relationships are considered role inappropriate and not conducive to dating or friendship relationships.

Does age really matter? When you're a teenager, yes. During adolescence, dating someone more than two years older or younger can be at the very least problematic or in the worst-case scenario, illegal, harmful, and dangerous. Consider the differences between the life experiences of someone in seventh grade and someone in twelfth grade. Think about how you have changed physically and emotionally in the last few years.

Your best bet for a safe and appropriate relationship is to date someone who is similar in age – usually within one to two years of your age. A more than two-year age difference may lead not only to minor misunderstandings but to major unrealistic or harmful expectations as well.

Various studies have shown that major age differences in teen dating relationships can cause major problems. One study showed that most teen mothers were impregnated by men approximately six years older. Why would a 22-year-old man want to date a 16-year-old girl? If he is a skilled groomer, he knows that a teen girl is much easier to manipulate and use than a woman his own age.

Looking for Balance

Remember that a healthy friendship or a dating relationship should always involve give and take from both people. That doesn't mean you should keep a scorecard of what you and your friends do for one another, but it is a good idea to see if there is a healthy balance. Evaluate the relationships you have now and try to find that balance. No one person should be in total control or do all of the taking. One person trying to dominate or control another is not a sign of friendship or true love. In fact it is just the opposite, a sign of imbalance and potential problems.

It's also good to keep in mind that friendship and dating are just one portion of life. Spending too much time thinking about one relationship takes away from all of the other important things you should be concentrating on. Make sure you take care of the responsibilities you have to your family, school, church, and community. Your friends should respect your choice to do so.

Realize that friendships and dating relationships will change; some will change for the better, some for the worse. Learn how to adjust to these changes without giving up the things you believe in. Strive to be flexible and understanding of others while sticking with the things you know are right.

Look at past relationships that were positive. Make a list of the things that made those relationships healthy. Identify any positive changes friends have helped you make in your life. Then name the things you do to help make positive changes in others. Always make sure you are encouraging one another to change for the better.

It may also help to examine relationships that didn't work out. Although relationships are a two-way street, try to figure out what part you played to make each relationship end up the way it did. Remember what you learned from past relationships so that you can avoid those mistakes in the future.

Friendship and Dating Skills

Webster's Dictionary defines a skill as an "ability, proficiency, or expertness that comes from training or practice." To describe people as "skilled" implies that they know what they're doing, that they have knowledge, competence, or experience in a given area. With education and practice you could become skilled at any number of things – computer programming, playing an instrument, playing soccer, or even sky diving.

Learning Skills

There are various kinds of skills you'll acquire throughout your lifetime – study skills, academic skills, athletic skills, job-related skills. Some of the most important skills you'll need to be successful in life are called social skills. Social skills enable you to have healthy and positive relationships – at home, at school, at work and in the broader community.

Like any other set of skills, social skills are abilities or behaviors obtained through education and practice. Social skills are the practical "how-tos" of relating and getting along with others. Some examples of social skills include:

How to greet someone/introduce yourself

How to ask for a date

How to make a request

How to accept "no" for an answer

How to accept criticism

How to accept consequences

How to disagree appropriately

How to resist peer pressure

How to say "no" effectively

How to resolve conflict

How to give and accept an apology

How to give and accept a compliment

How to engage in a conversation

How to solve problems

How to show respect

How to respect others' boundaries

How to use self-control

How to express feelings appropriately

How to ask for help

How to handle anger appropriately

How to handle sexuality appropriately

How to recognize and respond to those in need

How to interact appropriately with members of the other gender

How to express affection appropriately

You began learning social skills while you were still very young. You first learned them by observing and imitating how family members related to one another. As you got older, you began to use social skills with playmates and friends. Eventually you went to school where you learned and practiced even more social skills as you interacted with classmates and teachers. Most of you have been learning and practicing various social skills for many years now.

Some of you may already know how to do most of the skills listed above and some of you may still have a few to learn. What's most important is to keep using the social skills you already have while making an effort to learn and practice the skills you don't know. Learning and practicing social skills will help you improve the quality of all your relationships – with family, friends, classmates, co-workers, neighbors – and especially with the guys or girls you choose to date!

friendship and Dating

What do you want to be when you grow up? You've probably heard that question a hundred times! It **is** an important question to think about, especially when you are a teenager. **Now** is the time that you should begin to think about your future. Most of you are beginning to take a closer look at "life after graduation" – college, technical school, the military, or the workforce. Some of you have already taken classes or other steps toward preparing for your future educational and career-related goals.

When thinking about your future, have you ever asked yourself this question: What kind of relationships do you want to have later in life? Ten years from now, do you hope to be seriously dating someone or perhaps be married? Do you hope to be a parent someday? If so, what are you doing **right now** to prepare for those relationships? These may seem like strange questions, but think about it. Isn't preparing for future relationships just as important as preparing for your future career?

If you were to take a "marriage poll" among your friends and classmates, you'd probably discover that most teens hope to get married someday. Even though that "someday" will likely occur several years from now, marriage and parenthood are still goals for many teens. But is there any way to prepare for the relational goals of serious dating, marriage and family life? Is there anything you can be doing right now that will help you become a better dating partner, fiancé, spouse, or parent?

The good news is yes! There are things you can be doing right now that can help you prepare to have healthy and happy adult relationships. And it all begins with friendship. Learning how to be and have a friend is the best practice for marriage. In fact, friendship between spouses is the foundation for a good and lasting marriage. If your spouse is not first and foremost your friend, chances are slim that your marriage will last. Contrary to popular beliefs, it is good friendship skills, not sexual skills, that will help your marriage stand the test of time.

Characteristics of a Real Friend

There's a lot of talk today about "keeping it real." What does that mean when it comes to friendship? What are the characteristics of a **real** friend? Do you have what it takes? Examine your friendships in light of this list!

Real friendship is:

- **Reciprocal** – Both friends like one another and consider the other a friend.

- **Sharing** – Friends share common interests and experiences together, are there for each other during both good and bad times.

- **Inclusive** – Both have other friends; new friends are always welcome. The friendship is not exclusive.

- **Based on trust** – Friends rely on each other, stand up for each other, and keep their word.

- **Helpful** – A friend encourages you to do the right thing, never tempts you to do wrong or harmful things, helps you grow as a person.

- **Honest** – Friends tell the truth, even when it may be hard to do so.

- **Respectful** – Friends treat others with dignity, don't put down, control, bully, or manipulate others.

- **Caring** – A friend has the other person's best interests in mind.

Virtual Relationships

E-mail, computer chat rooms, and instant messaging have changed the way many people meet, relate, and communicate with others. The Internet can bring strangers together from all over the world. But it brings them together in "virtual reality." Remember virtual reality is just that – "virtual" – not **real.** Meeting and "talking" to someone on the Internet is very different from meeting and talking to someone face-to-face.

Think about it. Meeting and talking with someone face-to-face give you the chance to practice many important social skills – skills that can help you decide whether or not you'd like to get to know this person better. One such set of skills involves learning how to read and respond to social cues and body language. Face-to-face relating gives you the opportunity to learn how to observe and "read" body language.

Remember, we communicate both verbally, with words, and nonverbally, with our body – posture, facial expressions, eye contact, etc. In fact, the majority of human communication, more than 70 per cent, is done nonverbally. We usually learn more about people and what they are really trying to say from their body language and expressions than we do from their words.

You cannot observe social cues or body language in virtual reality. Because you cannot see nonverbal communication in computer screen messages, you severely limit what you can learn about the other person. Since you have such limited information – really only a typed message – it becomes nearly impossible to recognize and understand someone else's boundaries. And it becomes difficult for you to establish and communicate your boundaries as well. How do you know if what you are reading is true? How do you know if the other person is being honest about himself or herself? What do you have to base a real friendship on?

Perhaps you're not meeting new people on the Net, maybe you just like to e-mail, chat with, and instant message friends you already know. Are these ways of communicating affecting your friendship skills? Just remember, face-to-face relating is the best way to get to know or grow your friendship. Sometimes it may seem easier to "say" what's on your mind via the Net, but remember these dangers as well:

Once you send it – it's out there for others to read. There's a very real possibility that someone you don't want reading what you wrote will do just that. Never send something you wouldn't want your parents to read.

When we're angry or hurt we often say things we later regret. You may be tempted to "say" even more in an e-mail or instant message because you're not face-to-face. And you may end up doing more damage in the long run. Being face-to-face to talk about feelings or resolve conflicts will probably motivate you to use more self-control and better communication skills.

It becomes easier to ask or answer sexually suggestive or inappropriate questions because communicating via the Net is detached from reality and anonymous in nature. Don't go there. Don't reveal personal or sexual information about yourself to anyone on the Net – stranger or friend.

Strangers

Whether in cyberspace or face-to-face, you need to be able to differentiate between a stranger, acquaintance, companion, and friend.

In face-to-face relating, it's easy to identify strangers. They are people you have never met before. You don't know their names or anything else about them. As a young child, your parents taught you to avoid talking to or going anywhere with a stranger. They were teaching you good boundaries. They were teaching you how to protect yourself from getting used or abused.

The boundaries you learned about strangers as a child still apply today. It's still best to avoid talking to strangers, unless it's about superficial topics like sports, weather, or time of day. It's still a good idea to avoid going anywhere with a stranger.

But what about people you "talk" to on the Internet? The truth is **everyone** you first "meet" in cyberspace is a stranger, and boundary rules for strangers should apply.

Safe boundaries on the Internet are:

- **Don't chat with, e-mail, or instant message someone you have never met.**

- **Never share personal information on the Net.**

- **Avoid all conversations with sexual content.**

The problem for many teens today is that they aren't applying those healthy boundaries to Internet "relationships." They are chatting with and sometimes actually meeting and going places with strangers. Some teens are revealing personal information and having sexual conversations with complete strangers.

It's easy to see how it can happen. You start chatting with someone new. You chat every day for a few weeks. You chat about what you like, what you think, and how you feel on various subjects. It **seems** as if you are becoming friends. The problem is – you have no way of knowing whether or not any of it is "real." When you're chatting with someone on the Net, you actually know next to nothing about that person. All you really know is that he or she has access to a computer at that time. The person could be male, female, teen or adult, in your neighborhood or halfway around the world. Worse yet, that person could be up to no good. Sexual predators love the Internet. If offers them an anonymous and boundary-less environment – and easy access to those who are vulnerable and trusting.

Your best bet on the Internet is to avoid chatting, e-mailing, or messaging with someone you've never met in person. Only "talk" to people you know to be trustworthy. And when on the Net with people you do know, you should still refrain from sharing any personal information and avoid all conversations that have sexual content. It's the best way to protect yourself and your reputation.

Acquaintances and Companions

In face-to-face relating, acquaintances are people you have seen or met before. They are people you see occasionally. You may know their name, or that they go to your school or live in your neighborhood, but you know little else. Your time spent together is brief – a passing "hello" or a short conversation about math class. It's perfectly acceptable for acquaintances to have a brief conversation in a public place about superficial topics or work on a school project together in class, but it's best not to go anywhere alone with an acquaintance. Remember, an acquaintance is someone you don't know well. You haven't spent enough time nor learned enough about this person to tell whether or not this person is trustworthy or friendship material.

A companion is someone you know a little better. Perhaps you have several classes together, are neighbors, or work together. A companion is someone with whom you have had several longer face-to-face conversations and whom you have regular contact with – you participate in the same school club, play on the same sports team, work on community projects together, or play together in the neighborhood. Companions may share some limited personal information and feelings with one another. There is a deeper sense of trust and knowledge about one another.

Acquaintances and companions are people you spend **real time** with. It is while becoming an acquaintance or companion that you learn more about the other person and then decide whether or not you'd like to become friends. Without a real sense of trust, a true friendship cannot grow. And the only way real trust is developed is through face-to-face relating and spending time together. You can't rush it or fake it.

friends

Occasionally two people who are acquaintances or companions become friends. How? **Both people** identify qualities they like in the other person and choose to spend more time getting to know one another better. The key factor is **time** – real friendships grow over time, they don't happen overnight.

What's okay to talk to a friend about? Friends talk about what they have in common – likes, interests, school, job, music, sports, community, school, or church. Deeper thoughts and feelings should only be shared with a good friend who has proven trustworthy.

What's okay to do with a friend? Play a game, talk, watch sports, go for a walk, bake cookies, do a service project together, go swimming, shop, etc. What's not okay to do with a friend? Bullying, teasing, manipulating or using your friend in any way, especially not sexually! "Friends with favors" or "friends with privileges" are not friends at all. It's mutual use and nothing more.

The Dating Steps

Here's another interesting point – one that is often lost in contemporary society. Since friendship is the foundation for a good marriage – and dating is the means by which most people meet and decide whom to marry – then dating is really a form of friendship.

Dating, formerly called courtship, is not and never was intended to be a sexually intimate relationship. The purpose of dating is to learn how to be friends with and have fun with members of the other gender. And for many, the ultimate purpose of dating is to find a suitable spouse. There are seven steps to healthy dating.

STEP 1 Same-Gender Friendships

Do you remember the first time you tried to kick a soccer ball down the field, play a musical instrument, hit a baseball, or play a new video game? Learning to do any of these things doesn't happen overnight. It takes lots of practice, step by step, day after day, to become skilled at any of these activities.

Learning how to date is very similar. Just like a new soccer player whose first steps are taken while doing kicking drills or watching a coach's demonstration, there are some first steps and foundational skills you need to learn before you even start to date. These "first steps" will help you practice the skills you'll need to have healthy friendships and will lay the foundation for healthy relationships throughout your life.

Before you start dating, the first step is learning how to be and have friends of the same gender. Learning how to be a real friend is the basis for all relationships, especially dating relationships. Developing same-gender friendships gives you the opportunity to practice important social skills that you will need later when relating to members of the opposite gender. And, no matter what your age, you never outgrow the need for same-gender friendships.

If you have not learned how to be and have friends with others of your gender, your dating relationships will quickly get off track. It's never too late to change your focus and practice creating and maintaining healthy friendships with other guys or girls. You'll be glad you did!

STEP 2 Opposite-Gender Friendships

The second step of dating is also foundational – a step designed to help you continue to improve the friendship skills you developed in your same-gender friendships, but this time in a different kind of friendship – a totally platonic, non-sexual friendship with someone of the opposite sex! Many teens have discovered that they have more fun in school just being good friends together – hanging around and having fun in a group, without the pressure of "hooking up" or "getting serious."

There are some who think that men and women can never be "just friends," that sexual attraction will always get in the way. We wholeheartedly disagree. Friendship between men and women is not only possible, it is necessary – especially when a man and woman plan to marry!

There's no doubt that men and women are different – in many ways. And it is because we are so different that it is important to befriend one another. In such friendships, you can learn a lot not only about the other gender, but also about yourself, and ultimately about how to best communicate with, understand, and be friends with a future dating partner or spouse.

STEP 3 Friendly Dating

It is only when you have mastered the skills needed for the first two dating steps that you should proceed to Step 3. In order to participate in Step 3: Friendly Dating, you must be very clear about your own physical, emotional, sexual, and spiritual boundaries. And, you must be able to communicate these boundaries to those you will date.

The purpose of Step 3 is similar to Step 2 in that it gives you the chance to practice friendship skills with members of the other gender. But friendly dating can be even more than that. Friendly dating will most likely involve spending time with and practicing friendships skills with someone to whom you are attracted. For friendly dating to remain friendly – rather than hot and heavy – each person must maintain healthy physical and sexual boundaries.

Talk to your parents or another trusted adult about how far is far enough – how physically and sexually close you should get to someone you are friendly dating. We suggest going no further than hand holding or hugging when dating at this level. Maintaining clear boundaries regarding limited physical and sexual closeness can free you to really get to know one another and to practice the rules for good boundaries mentioned in the previous chapter. Limiting physical and sexual closeness helps you to develop important skills like saying and accepting "no," exhibiting sexual self-control, and respecting others' boundaries.

Friendly dating can happen in a group, on a double date, or as a single date. But it always implies that you are getting to know and going out with various members of the other gender. In other words, friendly dating is "dating around." It is **not** an exclusive relationship.

Dating Steps

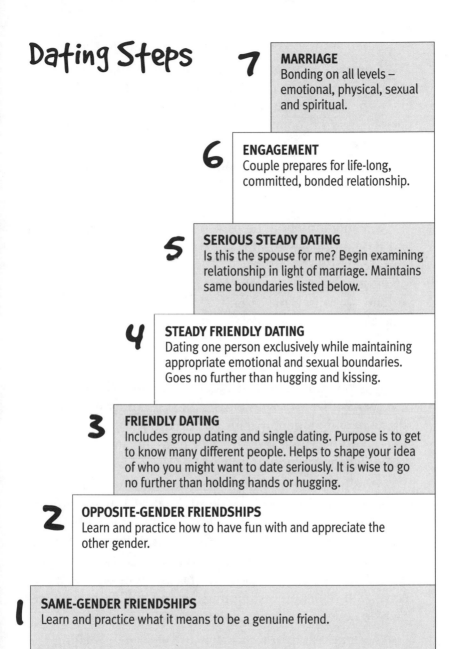

7 MARRIAGE
Bonding on all levels –
emotional, physical, sexual
and spiritual.

6 ENGAGEMENT
Couple prepares for life-long,
committed, bonded relationship.

5 SERIOUS STEADY DATING
Is this the spouse for me? Begin examining
relationship in light of marriage. Maintains
same boundaries listed below.

4 STEADY FRIENDLY DATING
Dating one person exclusively while maintaining
appropriate emotional and sexual boundaries.
Goes no further than hugging and kissing.

3 FRIENDLY DATING
Includes group dating and single dating. Purpose is to get
to know many different people. Helps to shape your idea
of who you might want to date seriously. It is wise to go
no further than holding hands or hugging.

2 OPPOSITE-GENDER FRIENDSHIPS
Learn and practice how to have fun with and appreciate the
other gender.

1 SAME-GENDER FRIENDSHIPS
Learn and practice what it means to be a genuine friend.

If you want to keep it friendly make sure to avoid:

Couple behavior – Exclusive dating, necking, exchanging gifts like jewelry, clothing or stuffed animals, only walking with, only talking to, or always thinking about this one person, writing romantic or sexual notes, hanging all over each other.

Grooming tactics – Jealousy and possessiveness, insecurity, intimidation, anger, accusation, bribery, flattery, status, or control.

Keeping it friendly helps you to keep your options open and date around without hurting or using others. It keeps your reputation clean and helps you steer clear of giving mixed messages. It enables you to meet, get to know, and perhaps even become friends with several people of the opposite gender while avoiding messy and painful breakups.

STEP 4 Steady Friendly Dating

It is possible that while friendly dating you may meet one person that you would like to get to know even better. After a period of friendly dating of this person and others, the two of you decide to friendly date only one another. This is Step 4: Steady Friendly Dating.

Most high school teens are not and should not be thinking about marriage yet. They know that they have more to learn, experience, and achieve in life before they'll be ready to marry. They know they are not yet ready for Step 5 – not yet ready to be asking the question "Is this the spouse for me?" Yet, rather than dating several different people, a few teens, with their parents' permission and guidance, may feel ready to develop a deeper friendship with one person.

It is important to stress that in this type of dating the temptation to go "too far" sexually will most likely increase. Because the amount of time spent together increases and because the two are most likely developing a closer emotional connection, the desire to be physically closer will also grow. We recommend the same physical and sexual boundaries for this step as for the previous dating step. Though it will probably be more difficult now, teens that date at this step need to hold fast to clear and firm physical and sexual boundaries. Maintaining and respecting boundaries will help protect each person from going too far too fast.

Teens who are ready for this Dating Step 4 are teens who demonstrate the following skills – they are able to set and communicate clear boundaries and limits, have self-control, are able to resist peer pressure, can handle their sexuality and frustration appropriately, can express feelings appropriately, and show self-respect and respect for others.

It is extremely important that teens involved in serious steady friendly dating do not limit themselves to spending time **only** with their boyfriend or girlfriend. Now more than ever before, these teens need to spend a good amount of time with other male and female friends, as well as with family, so that their boundaries remain firm and priorities clear.

Situations to **avoid** that will help you keep healthy sexual boundaries while steady friendly dating include:

- Too much time alone together

- Visual sexual stimulation – movies, music, music videos, games, Internet sites, etc., with sexual content

- Sexually suggestive clothing

- "Bump and grind" style of dancing

- Drug or alcohol use

- Going anywhere or doing anything you can't tell your parents about

It is also extremely important that teens involved in steady dating realize that there is a high breakup rate for this kind of relationship. Most teen couples who steady date in high school do **not** end up married. Most will break up. And "breaking up is hard to do."

This should tell us something very important about friendship and dating skills. If you keep the focus on friendship (Dating Steps 1-3) and hold firm to healthy physical, emotional, and sexual boundaries in all your relationships, you are more likely to avoid the pain, loss, and embarrassment of gut-wrenching breakups.

STEP 5 Serious Steady Dating

This type of dating relationship is **not** for high school teens. It is developmentally appropriate for late teens, young adulthood and beyond. It is in this dating step when you begin to ask yourself: Is this the spouse for me? Do I really love this person? Does he or she really love me? It is at this step that the couple begins to examine the relationship in light of marriage.

All the skills listed above are necessary for this level of dating. Just as in steady friendly dating, it is extremely important to maintain clear and appropriate sexual, emotional, physical and spiritual boundaries so that each person can make good decisions about the future of the relationship.

STEP 6 Engagement

At this time, the couple begins preparing to create and share a life together. Discussions about finances, in-laws, conflict resolution, child-rearing, etc., need to happen now. The focus should be on preparing for the future, not just for the wedding day.

Again, it is very important for the couple to set and maintain clear and firm boundaries. The temptation to go further sexually will resurface and become stronger. Remember, engagement is **not** the same as marriage. Many engagements **do not** result in marriage. Now is **not** the time to relax your boundaries.

STEP 7 Marriage

For most people, marriage is the ultimate goal of dating. If all the previous steps have been followed, friendship skills have been mastered, each have maintained appropriate boundaries, and a real love for and commitment to the other person exists, then the couple will have an excellent chance of achieving a lasting, loving marriage.

Summary

Relationships are not random. Who we befriend and date are not accidents of fate. When it comes to relating, and especially dating, there are choices and decisions to be made long before we ever meet that special person. Knowing yourself, understanding what makes for a good or a bad relationship, being sure of your values and boundaries, and practicing good social skills will set the stage for healthy friendships and dating relationships now and in the future.

All this thought and preparation may seem less than romantic. But try thinking about it this way – it is within healthy relationship boundaries that a real and lasting romance can flourish.